**THIS BOOK
BELONGS TO:**

big food
for wee macs

fiona armstrong

ANGELS' SHARE®

The Angels' Share is an imprint of
Neil Wilson Publishing Ltd
303 The Pentagon Centre
36 Washington Street
GLASGOW
G3 8AZ

Tel: 0141-221-1117
Fax: 0141-221-5363
E-mail: info@nwp.co.uk
www.angelshare.co.uk
www.nwp.co.uk

A catalogue record for this book is available from the British Library.

ISBN 1-903238-19-6
Typeset in Bosis
Printed in Spain by Artes Graficas Elkar

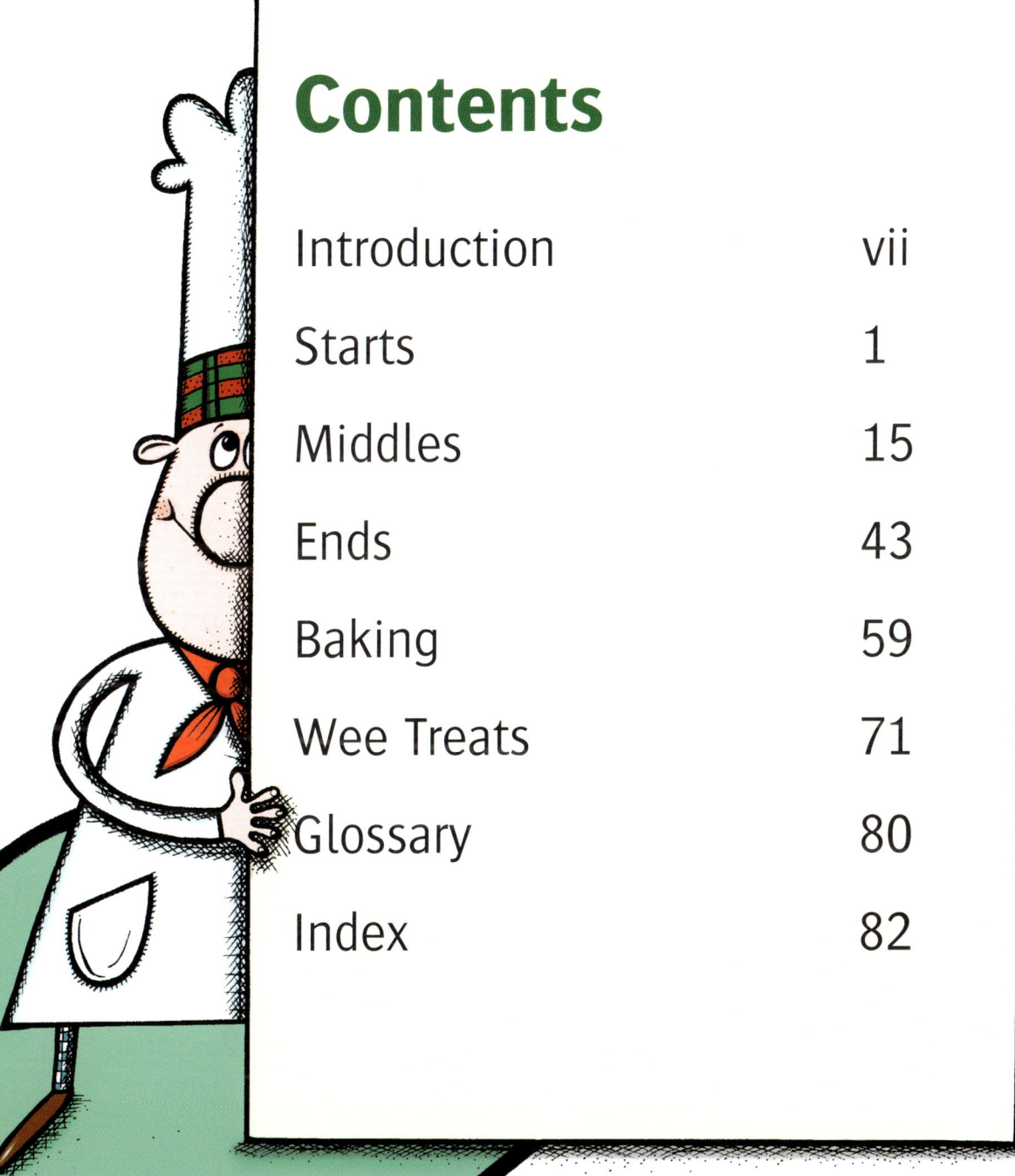

Contents

Introduction   vii

Starts   1

Middles   15

Ends   43

Baking   59

Wee Treats   71

Glossary   80

Index   82

INTRODUCTION

'THE BEST BIT IS LICKING THE BOWL'

We love food and we love cooking. My daughter, Natasha, and I always seem to have a house full of young and old and they're always hungry. From the gathering, to the preparation, to the eating ... the trick is to put something yummy on the table.

'PICKING BRAMBLES ... IT WAS EAT ONE, PUT ONE IN THE BASKET'

We live in the countryside and can pick some food ourselves. But trips to the supermarket can also be fun, especially if you're prepared to experiment. Go on, put a round, fat haggis or a packet of smoked fish into your trolley – you never know until you try it!

We did try Natasha's red pepper. It started as a seed at Guides and was eventually ripened in the greenhouse. We ate it with great ceremony on a crunchy cheese and lettuce salad. We also fried in butter and lemon the wee trout she caught in a Highland loch. Delicious! The first thing we ever made were pancakes – we began by carefully breaking eggs into a bowl, then speeded up as the milk and flour were whisked in – and finally there was the party atmosphere, as the pancakes were well and truly tossed.

'IT'S COOL TO COOK.'

Of course, we eat different things at different times. Soup and egg dishes are good when you're feeling under the weather. And if you want to party, you may fancy a tangy pizza. We need food to grow from wee to big macs – and though you may not be able to cook it all when you're small, you'll definitely want to eat it.

Though you'll probably start with things that you know (French Toast, Mince 'n' Tatties), most Wee Macs will experiment a little. In our house, we moved quickly from the bland to the exotic; from a mild cheese spread to a smelly Italian blue; from fish fingers to fresh tuna. That's why there are some strong tastes in the book – go on – give them a try!

Scottish food – it's about local ingredients like fish, potatoes, cheese, oats and fruit; it's about amazing dishes with real flavour. And with a growing interest worldwide in all things Scottish, there's a sense of achievement to be able to put a tartan tasty on the table.

'PUT ON YOUR PINNY'

Fast food is fine — but your own can be better. So come on Wee Macs, put on your pinny, get out your bowl and get your hands in there (washed first, of course). Let's make some really BIG FOOD and get mixing, stirring, beating, heating, rolling, filling, frying and mashing!

We've kept the portions small, but if there's a big tribe at home, you can always double the ingredients to make more. Nibbly things go down well, as does finger food. Puddings are always big favourites ("What's for afters, Mum?") and the Scots do like their sugar. They like their salt, too and serve their porridge with mountains of the stuff. We have used a little salt in some of the recipes — but we always use low-salt. Maybe you should too.

'BE BOLD, BE BRAVE!'

OK, there are a few recipes that won't win any prizes for healthy eating (Deep-Fried Mars Bars?) ... but the basic Scottish foods that we use — the oats, fish, cheese, fruit, vegetables — ARE good for you. Some of the recipes won't need supervision, but do be careful of the ones that involve using a stove or hot oil. It's boring, I know, but there are a few guidelines to follow on the next page.

THE WEE MAC'S KITCHEN

Children should always be supervised by an adult when cooking. Read the recipe. A hundred grams is not a thousand grams! If something needs frying at high temperature, always let the grown-up do it. Wear oven gloves when picking up something hot or putting things in and out of the oven. Keep saucepan handles to the side, in case someone knocks them off the stove. Remember that most things need to be watched or stirred; so don't go on the Game Boy and forget about the time. Watch out for knives – they need to be sharp to cut properly and safely, but be careful with those fingers; hold them with the sharp point pointing downwards and always use a chopping board! Care should also be taken with other sharp kitchen utensils like graters, scissors and peelers. Make sure hands are dry before switching machines like processors and electric whisks on and off. Wipe up spills as they happen so nobody ends up slipping. Turn off stoves and cookers when you're finished and, best of all, remember to wash up...

So be bold, be brave – pop the prune in the Cock-a-Leekie, give more of a curry kick to the Kedgeree, imagine you're building muscles with an Irn Bru Mousse. In our house, we've had all the disasters you can think of – the cakes that wouldn't rise, the biscuits that burned and the pie that fell on the floor. Don't worry! Start today and make some Big Food for Wee Macs.

Fiona Armstrong
February 2004

Dedicated to my lovely Tashie, who cooked and tasted.

STARTS

Finger food is much more fun than using a knife and fork – but you won't wipe your hands down your jeans afterwards, will you? Or worse still down the side of the chair!

Bits 'n' Pieces is one of our favourite quick snacks; just take a bit of cooked chopped meat, add some chopped apple and tomato, a handful of nuts and a few slithers of Scottish cheddar cheese; sit a few oat biscuits on the side and you have perfect Wee Mac food. But if you want to be more adventurous, you have to put on a pinny, get out the weighing scales and start creating.

Keep it small and keep it tasty. That's the secret. This section has recipes for great snack food – in fact it's all you need for a party with a Scottish theme. Take some Smoked Salmon Wheels and a plateful of cheesy Mini Mac Pies. Add a bowl of Smoked Mackerel Creamy, lay out some Oatie Chicken Drummers and 'See You Jimmy' Heids and the fun will begin. All you need now is a kilt. If you can't play the bagpipes, get hold of a song called 'Donald Where's Yer Troosers' – that will get everyone into the swing of things.

Pizza Oaties

Oatcakes are as Scottish as they come: for a multicultural snack, top them like a pizza and see Scotland meet Italy on your plate! For speed, use ready-made pasta sauce from a jar, but you can make your own.

(Serves 4)

8 Scottish oatcake biscuits
4 tbsp tomato pasta sauce
50g/2oz finely grated parmesan

Divide the sauce between the biscuits. Sprinkle with the cheese.

Place under a hot grill for a minute, or until the cheese melts. Remove carefully, so the biscuits don't break up.

Cool a little before serving.

Tomato Sauce

1 can of tinned tomatoes
1 small clove garlic, crushed
1 small onion, grated
1 tbsp vegetable oil
1/4 tsp dried oregano

Fry the onion in the oil until soft. Then add all the other ingredients. Squash the tomatoes with a wooden spoon or better still, a masher, and simmer until there's no more liquid.

Allow to cool before using.

WEE NOTES

4

Smoked Salmon Wheels

Yes, smoked salmon is a bit sophisticated ... but expensive habits can be acquired at an early age ...

(Serves 4)

4 large thin slices brown bread
50g/2oz soft butter
110g/4 slices smoked salmon, enough to cover the bread

Cut the crusts off the bread, butter each slice and lay the smoked salmon on top, dividing it equally.

Starting at the narrowest side of the bread, firmly roll up each slice like a Swiss roll. Then cover and put in the fridge for an hour.

When ready, take out of the fridge and cut each roll into $1\frac{1}{2}$ centimetre 'wheels'.

WEE NOTES

Tattie Hash Waffles

The Scots are great ones for frying food in batter – and these are yummy – but if you're cooking together make sure it's the adult who deals with the hot oil. If you don't like corned beef, you can add some minced chicken or other meat instead.

(Serves 4)

225g/8oz mashed potato
110g/4oz mashed corned beef
50g/2oz plain flour
1 egg
150 ml/¼ pint of milk
Salt and pepper
Vegetable oil for frying

Mix the potato and corned beef and season with salt and pepper. In another bowl, make the batter by whisking together the flour, egg, milk and a pinch of salt. Make sure you have no lumps.

Pour 4cm of oil into a saucepan and slowly start to heat it. The oil is hot enough at 180° C (test by adding a small cube of bread to the pan. It should turn golden after a minute). Take heaped teaspoons of the potato mix, round them with your hand, then dip them in the batter and fry three at a time for a minute or two.

When ready they should be slightly puffed and browned. Make savoury pancakemen from any leftover batter (see page 52).

WEE NOTES

Smoked Mackerel Creamy

Smoked fish gives a real flavour of Scotland. For a special touch, serve in hollowed-out sections of cucumber or tomato. Mixing it with the cheeses gives a light, creamy taste.

(Serves 4–6)

225g/8oz boneless smoked mackerel fillets
110g/4oz cream cheese
110g/4oz cottage cheese
Juice of half a lemon
Salt and pepper

Skin the mackerel and mash with the cream and cottage cheeses. Now add the lemon juice and season with salt and pepper.

Alternatively, place everything in a processor and whizz for a few seconds.

Oatcakes, fingers of toast, or sticks of carrot, celery and red peppers go down well with this.

WEE NOTES

'See You Jimmy' Heids

'See You Jimmy' is a real Glaswegian, complete with red hair and a tammy. These egg-heads will make everyone laugh at tea-time!

(Serves 4)

4 eggs
1 x 180g tin tuna, drained
2 tbsp mayonnaise
2 small gherkins
1 small tomato
2 medium carrots, peeled
1 midget gem lettuce

Place the eggs in a pan of water, bring to the boil and simmer for four minutes. Then cool in cold water, peel and halve lengthways.

WEE NOTES

Take out the yolks and mix them with the tuna and mayonnaise. Spoon this mixture back into the egg whites, smoothing it out so it covers the tops completely.

Cut the gherkins to use for eyes and a nose, and the tomato to form a mouth. Grate the carrot into long, coarse strips and use that to make the 'hair' of the head. Use the lettuce to make a green collar for his shirt.

A Tam O' Shanter is optional!

Mini Mac Pies

Macaroni Cheese Pies are a great Scottish favourite. These mini versions will disappear very quickly! You can make bigger-sized bread cases – just double the quantities and feed the left-over bread to the birds ...

(Serves 4)

6 large slices bread
50g/2oz dried macaroni
50g/2oz cheddar cheese, grated
50g/2oz butter
150 ml/1/4 pint milk
2 flat tsp plain flour
Salt and pepper

Pre-heat the oven to Gas Mark 6/200° C.
Melt half the butter and using a pastry brush, grease a 12-cup canapé tin.

Each cup should be 5 cm/2 inch across the top. Now cut the crusts off the bread and with a rolling pin, roll the slices flat. Take a 6 cm/2½ inch round cutter and cut two circles from each slice.

Carefully but firmly push the bread circles into the greased tin cups and brush with melted butter. Bake in the oven for five minutes, or until golden.

Meanwhile, bring a large pan of water to the boil. Add a little salt, tip in the macaroni and cook according to the instructions on the packet. Drain in a colander.

While the macaroni cooks, melt the remaining butter in a pan. Add the flour and cook for a few seconds. Remove the pan from the heat and whisk in the milk. Put back on the heat and, whisking all the time, simmer until you have a thickened, lump-free sauce. Add the grated cheese, season with salt and pepper and stir in the cooked macaroni.

Cool slightly, then put teaspoonfuls of the mixture into the cooked bread cases. Serve at once, before they get soggy!

WEE NOTES

Auld Alliance/French Toast

The Auld Alliance goes back hundreds of years, to the days when France sided with Scotland against the English. Some Scottish recipes originate from the French royal court. But French Toast is not at all posh. It's comfort food and you can eat it sweet or savoury.

(Serves 4)

4 eggs, beaten
Salt and pepper
50g/2oz butter
8 slices white bread

Beat the eggs and season with a little salt and pepper. Put a frying pan onto a low heat and melt a quarter of the butter. When it starts to fizzle, dip two slices of the bread into the egg mixture and coat on both sides. Cook in the pan for a minute on each side. Repeat with the rest of the butter and egged bread.

Serve with tomato sauce. For a sweet version, leave out the salt and pepper and serve with syrup.

WEE NOTES

Nourishing Soup

This is great food for anyone who's feeling under the weather. Our friend Malcolm's granny always made 'nourishing soup' in times of sickness or crisis. If my daughter is tired or starting a cold she always asks for nourishing soup.

570 ml/1pint water
2 vegetable stock cubes
3 heaped tbsp red lentils
1 onion, finely chopped
1 carrot, finely chopped

Heat the water and add the stock cubes.

When the cubes are dissolved, add the lentils, carrots and onion and stir. Bring to the boil, then cover and simmer for half an hour.

Season with salt and pepper and, if it's too thick, add a little milk or cream.

WEE NOTES

MIDDLES

This can be the tricky bit. Yes, you may like to live on chips – and the Scots will fry anything, even pizzas, but imagine being able to make a meal that makes everyone sit up and say, 'is there any more?' In the old days, I used to mix the meat with the pudding if my daughter wouldn't eat it. I can't do that now she's 11 … what a shame!

So, let's make something delicious! Make your taste buds really tingle and add some more curry powder to the Kid's Kedgeree. Live dangerously and fill the Nest of Neeps with haggis instead of egg. Go mad with potatoes: the Scots, like the Irish, love their tatties and you can fry them, bake them or boil them, then mix them with cheese or meat – whatever takes your fancy.

It'll all be delicious. Just remember that you're dealing with hot stoves and hot oil, so do be careful. Remember, also, not to make the portions too big, as there's nothing worse than being faced with a huge plateful you know you won't eat … and then someone will say, 'When I was your age, I'd have got it for breakfast' – or worse still, 'Just think of all the starving children in the world.' Oh no!

And a tip for adults: when you serve up, try to keep different foods separate on the plate – and don't try to hide anything risky like onions because they'll always be found!

Kid's Kedgeree

Kedgeree is a type of Indian dish eaten in Scotland during the 19th century for breakfast or supper. If you're cooking for Real Big Macs, add more curry powder! I've used quails' eggs because they're small, but they can be hard to get hold of. Four ordinary eggs will do just as well – just chop them into quarters.

(Serves at least 4)

12 quails' eggs
25g/1oz butter
1 tbsp olive oil
1 onion, peeled and chopped
175g/6oz long grain white rice
425 ml/$^3/_4$ pint vegetable or chicken stock
Half a teaspoon curry powder
350g/12oz boned smoked haddock, cut into half-inch pieces
150 ml/$^1/_4$ pint single cream or milk

1 lemon, sliced
1 tablespoon chopped parsley

Put the quails' eggs gently in a pan, bring to the boil and simmer for two minutes, then put into cold water, cool, peel and halve.

Melt the butter and oil and cook the onion slowly until golden and soft. Then add the rice and stir round. Pour in the stock, add the curry powder, stir again and bring to the boil. Simmer, uncovered, for approximately 12–15 minutes. The rice needs to be five minutes away from being ready to eat, so check the cooking time on the packet.

Sit the pieces of haddock on top of the rice, pour over the cream, put back the lid and simmer for a further five minutes. Divide carefully between dishes and place the halved eggs on top. Squeeze on some lemon and sprinkle on a bit of parsley.

WEE NOTES

WEE NOTES

White Neep Salad

Neeps are turnips – usually the yellow ones you eat with haggis. The small white ones can be as sweet as apples and are generally gobbled up.

(Serves 4)

3 small white turnips
1 medium carrot
110g/4oz lightly cooked chopped green vegetable – eg green beans
1 tbsp olive oil
2 tsp lemon juice
Salt and pepper

Peel and coarsely grate the turnips. Mind your fingers on the grater! Peel and grate the carrot. Mix the turnip and carrot carefully with the green vegetables and toss everything gently in the olive oil and lemon juice. Season with salt and pepper.

Oatie Drummers

This is another basic Scottish food. Oats are very good for you, though you might not eat them now that you know that!

(Serves 4)

8 chicken drumsticks
1 egg
110g/4oz medium oats
50g/2oz plain flour
Salt and pepper

Heat the oven to Gas mark 6/200° C.
Grease a baking sheet.

In one bowl, season the flour with a little salt and pepper. In another, beat the egg. Put the oats into a third dish. Now dip the chicken drumsticks first in the flour, then in the beaten egg, and finally, roll them in the oats.

Place the chicken drumsticks on the greased baking sheet and bake in the oven for 35 minutes, or until cooked through.

WEE NOTES

Mince 'n' Tatties

This is always a great favourite in our house. It's another tasty comfort food for a cold day – and it's so easy to make.

(Serves 4-6)

1 large onion, peeled and finely chopped
1 large carrot, peeled and finely chopped
350g/12oz minced Scotch beef
425 ml/$^3/_4$ pint beef stock
450g/1lb potatoes, peeled and chopped into half-inch cubes

1 tbsp vegetable oil
1 tbsp plain flour
2 tbsp water
Salt and pepper

Heat the oil in a saucepan. Add the chopped carrot and onion and stir for a minute or so. Add the meat and stir until it's browned. Put in the stock and bring to the boil. Cover and simmer for 20 minutes.

Add the chopped potatoes, stir, cover again and cook for a further 15 minutes.

Mix the flour in a cup with the water, making sure you have no lumps. Add this to the meat and potatoes and carefully stir. Cook for a few minutes until the gravy thickens.

Season with salt and pepper and serve in soup bowls with slices of French bread.

WEE NOTES

Stovies

More of the Auld Alliance ... 'Stove' comes from the French 'etuve', which means 'stew' — and, of course, your stove is your cooker. In the Highlands, stovies are made with milk. In Glasgow, stovies with meat are known as 'High Heelers'. For Harvest stovies, leave out the bacon and use 6oz/175g grated cheese instead.

(Serves 4-6)

900g/2lb potatoes, peeled and thinly sliced
50g/2oz butter
110g/4oz bacon bits, all fat removed
150 ml/$\frac{1}{4}$ pint vegetable stock
Salt and pepper

Heat the oven to Gas Mark 4/180˚ C.
Use a little of the butter to grease a shallow baking dish.

Put a layer of sliced potatoes in the baking dish and sprinkle over a little salt and pepper — but be careful as the bacon and stock will already be salty. Add a few slithers of butter and some bacon bits. Continue layering the potatoes, butter and bacon. Finish with a layer of potatoes and a bit of butter. Pour over the stock, cover with a lid or foil and bake in the oven for about an hour, or until the potatoes are nearly cooked.

Remove the lid or foil and cook for another 15 minutes or so, to crisp and brown the top.

WEE NOTES

Red and White Salad

Cabbage is easy to grow and can stand a cold Scottish winter, but it's not everyone's dream food. Presented this way, crunchy and colourful, it's a bit more exciting.

(Serves 4)

110g/4oz red cabbage
110g/4oz hard white cabbage
2 sweet apples
2 tbsp mayonnaise
1 tbsp milk

Remove the outer skin and any tough core from the cabbages and shred them thinly – watch your fingers! Peel, core and grate the apples and mix everything in a bowl. Add the mayonnaise and milk and mix. Season with salt and pepper.

WEE NOTES

Rumbledethumps

Try it for the name, if nothing else! Like the Irish, the Scots once lived mainly on potatoes, or tatties. Champit tatties (mashed potatoes) and tattie soup were popular. The Highland version of this dish is Clapshot, while on the Scottish border, it's known as Rumbledethumps.

(Serves 4-6)

450g/1lb potatoes, peeled, cooked and mashed
50g/2oz butter, melted
250g/8oz cooked, chopped carrot, cabbage or peas
Salt and pepper
2 tbsp vegetable oil

Mix together the mashed potatoes, melted butter and chopped vegetables. Taste and season with salt and pepper.

Heat the oil in a frying pan and fry the mixture in spoonfuls. Brown on both sides for a few minutes.

Serve with baked beans for a really filling meal.

WEE NOTES

Children's Cock-a-Leekie

Liquidise the leeks to hide them, but if they are popular in your house, leave them whole. The prunes will cause some fun at the table, even if nobody eats them.

WEE NOTES

(Serves 4–6)

2 chicken breasts, skinned
570 ml/1 pint vegetable or chicken stock
2 large leeks, peeled, cleaned and chopped
250g/9oz potatoes, peeled and
chopped into small pieces
4 ready-to-eat prunes
Salt and pepper
Chopped parsley

Put the chicken breasts and stock into a pan. Bring to the boil and simmer for 20 minutes. Remove the chicken from the stock, cool slightly and cut into bite-sized pieces.

Add the chopped leeks and potatoes to the stock, put back on the stove and bring to the boil. Simmer for 15 minutes, then take off the heat, cool slightly and liquidise.

Put the soup back in the pan, add the chicken bits and gently reheat. Serve parsley separately. If you're feeling brave, float a prune on the top.

Wee Meaty Macs

Now, where would we be without the good old beefburger? Some might say a lot better off – but you can't beat home-made!

(Serves 4)

1 tsp vegetable oil
400g/14oz Scotch beef
1 small onion, finely chopped
1 handful parsley, finely chopped
1 large carrot, peeled and grated
1 egg
Salt

8 small bread rolls
2 tbsp mayonnaise
8 small gherkins, sliced in half
A midget gem lettuce, shredded
2 small tomatoes, sliced

Set the oven to Gas Mark 4/180° C.
Grease a large baking tray with the oil.

With your hands, mix the meat, onion, parsley, carrot and egg in a bowl. Stir in a quarter of a teaspoon of salt, divide the mixture into eight rounds and flatten them out slightly. Rub them on one side across the oil on the tray and then turn them over – you want both sides of the burger to be oiled.

Bake for 20 minutes, or until cooked through, then remove from the oven. Allow to cool slightly.

Cut open the rolls, spread them with mayonnaise and add some gherkin, lettuce and tomato.

Put a burger in each roll and serve.

WEE NOTES

Neeps 'n' Tattie Nests

Bashed neeps and tatties (turnips and potatoes) are traditionally eaten with haggis. The 'Great Pudding of the Chieftain Race', as Robbie Burns called the haggis, is made of, how can we put it, bits from the inside of a sheep. It can be a bit strong, so this is a good alternative.

(Serves 4)

450g/1lb potatoes, peeled and cooked
225g/8oz yellow turnip, peeled and cooked
50g/2oz butter
4 eggs
Salt and pepper

(Serves 4)

Pre-heat the oven to Gas Mark 5/190° C.
Use a slither of the butter to grease 4 x 13 cm/5 inch ramekin dishes.

Mash the potato and turnip together until smooth. Melt the remaining butter and stir it in. Season with salt and pepper and divide the mixture between the dishes.

With the back of a spoon, make a well in the centre of the potato mix and break an egg into each.

Put into the oven for about 12 minutes, or until the eggs are cooked.

WEE NOTES

Tottie Fish Suppers

More fish! It's brain food, especially oily fish like salmon. If you can't catch your own, tinned fish is fine. Remember if you're cooking together the adult should do the frying,

(Serves 4)

3fl oz/75 ml milk
2 tbsp plain flour
2 eggs
225g/8oz cooked, boned salmon
Salt and pepper
2 tbsp vegetable oil for frying
1 lemon

Mix the milk and flour until smooth. Beat in the eggs. Flake the salmon and add that to the mixture. Season with a little salt and pepper.

Heat the oil in a frying pan and drop in tablespoons of the mixture. Cook for a couple of minutes on each side, or until golden brown.

WEE NOTES

Drain on kitchen paper and serve with a squeeze of lemon.

Wee Scotch Eggs

These are usually made with hen's eggs and breadcrumbs, but here we've used tiny quails' eggs and the more traditional oatmeal. If you can't get quails' eggs, use four normal ones instead.

(Serves 4)

12 quails' eggs
1 tbsp plain flour
Salt and pepper
1 hen's egg, beaten
350g/12oz pork sausage meat
50g/2oz medium oatmeal

Oil for frying OR
Set the oven at Gas Mark 5/190° C.

Put the quails' eggs into a pan of water, bring to the boil and simmer for three minutes. Then cool in cold water and carefully shell.

Put the flour in a bowl and season with salt and pepper. In another bowl break and beat the hen's egg. Put the oatmeal in a third bowl. Divide the sausage meat into 12 portions and press each bit out with your hand (if you're using large eggs you only need four portions of meat).

Put a little flour on your hands. Take a quails' egg and roll it in the flour. Cover it completely with a portion of meat. Then roll it in the beaten egg and finally in the oatmeal. Keep your hands floured or they'll become sticky.

Repeat with the remaining eggs. Then either fry the eggs in hot fat for a few minutes until the meat is cooked, or – for a healthier version – wrap loosely in foil and bake on a tray in the oven for 15-20 minutes.

Cut carefully into halves and serve hot or cold.

WEE NOTES

Cheese Patties

Patties get this name because you can pat them round with your hands. Like play-doh, they can be made into any shape you want. So get those hands in there!

(Serves 4)

450g/1lb potatoes, boiled and mashed
110g/4oz grated cheese
1 egg
110g/4oz medium oatmeal
25g/1oz parmesan cheese
1 tsp vegetable oil
Salt and pepper

Set the oven to Gas Mark 5/190° C.
Use the oil to grease a large baking tray.

Mix the mashed potato and grated cheese in one bowl. Add salt and pepper if needed. Mix the parmesan and oatmeal in another bowl.

With your hands, form the potato mix into 10 flattish rounds or 'patties'. Dip these into the beaten egg, then cover with the parmesan and oatmeal mix.

WEE NOTES

Put the patties on the tray and bake for about 20 minutes, or until crisp and golden on the outside.

Green Champit

Want to bring some colour to your plate? This dish will! If your tatties are chappit or champit, they're mashed. This is delicious served with slices of grilled Scottish bacon.

(Serves 4 – 6)

450g/1lb potatoes, peeled and chopped
250g/8oz frozen peas
50g/2oz butter
Salt and pepper

Put the potatoes in a pan, add a little salt, cover with water and boil until soft. In another pan, cover the peas with water and boil for three minutes.

Drain the potatoes, cool slightly and put in the food processor with the butter. Drain the peas, add them and process until completely smooth. See if it needs salt and pepper and serve. If you don't have a processor, you can always mash everything, but it won't be completely smooth.

WEE NOTES

Sit There Pie

Thanks to Gretna's Bruce Graham for this one. It was given this name in his house as everyone had to sit there until it was finished! Which is unfair, as it's absolutely delicious and is also a great way to use up leftovers.

(Serves 4)

25g/1oz butter
1 tbsp plain flour
300 ml/½ milk
110g/4oz chopped cooked vegetables – peas/carrots/broccoli, etc
200g/6oz chopped cooked meat – pheasant/chicken/ham
Salt and pepper
110g/4oz fresh breadcrumbs
50g/2oz grated cheese

Set the oven at Gas Mark 6/200° C.
Lightly grease four 13 cm/5 inch rameken dishes.

Melt the butter in a pan, add the flour and cook for a few seconds. Remove from the heat and whisk in the milk. Put back on the heat and cook, whisking all the time, until you have a smooth white sauce. Add salt and pepper to taste, then stir in the vegetables and the meat.

Divide the meaty sauce between the greased dishes. Mix the breadcrumbs with the grated cheese and sprinkle over the top.

Bake in the oven for about 15 minutes, or until heated through and browned on top.

WEE NOTES

Roastit Bubblyjock with Barley

I think this name dates back to Victorian times ... perhaps 'bubbly jock' is the noise a turkey makes. Like oats, barley is very Scottish. If barley isn't popular in your house, try Green Champit instead (see page 33).

(Serves 6)

1 x 1kg/2lb small turkey joint
110g/4oz butter
125 ml/^{3}/$_4$ pint chicken or vegetable stock
1 small onion, peeled and finely chopped
50g/2oz pearl barley
1 tbsp flour
1 tbsp chopped parsley
1 tbsp cranberry jelly
Salt and pepper

Pre-heat the oven to Gas Mark 6/200˚ C.

WEE NOTES

Sit the turkey on a length of foil, season with salt and pepper and spread half the butter over the top. Cover with the foil and cook in the oven for about an hour. You need approximately 25 minutes cooking for each 450g/1lb.

While that's cooking, melt the remaining butter in a pan and add the chopped onion. Put in the barley and stir. Pour over 275 ml/$^{1}/_{2}$ pint of the stock, cover with a lid and simmer for 30 minutes or until the barley is tender. You want the grains to be cooked, but still have some 'bite'. If it looks like it's becoming too dry, add a little water.

When the turkey's ready, take it from the oven, drain the juices into a pan and put the turkey in a warm place.

To make the gravy: add the remaining stock to the turkey juices and bring to the boil. Mix the flour with a couple of tablespoons of water until you have a smooth paste and add this to the pan, stirring all the time. Stir in the cranberry jelly and simmer for a minute or so.

Mix the barley with the chopped parsley. Serve the turkey slices with a spoonful of barley and the cranberry gravy.

Serve with carrots or peas.

Haggis Tatties

Fair fa' your honest, sonsie face,
Great chieftain o' the puddin'-race
Aboon them a' ye tak your place

Young and old, we love haggis in our house. The grown-ups might eat it with cream and a splash of whisky. For now, it's delicious in a buttery potato.

(Serves 4)

4 medium baking potatoes
110g/4oz cooked haggis
110g/4oz cooked mashed yellow turnip
50g/2oz butter
2 tbsp milk

Set the oven to Gas Mark 6/200° C.

Prick the potatoes with a fork and bake for an hour, or until soft.

Remove from the oven, allow to cool slightly and cut in half.

Use a spoon to scoop the cooked potato from the shells. Mix this with the haggis and mashed turnip. Melt the butter and mix that in, along with the milk.

Pile the mixture back into the shells and put back in the oven to heat for 10 minutes or so.

WEE NOTES

MY OWN MIDDLES RECIPE

ENDS

This is the best bit of all. One girl we knew used to lick her finger and wipe it all over a particularly delicious-looking pudding or cake. 'That one's mine!' she'd say. It usually was after that.

Most Wee Macs like to cook and eat sweet things – who can blame them? – and I've tried to use things that have a Scottish sound. I haven't included the famous Jeddard Snail, which is a sweet that comes from the Scottish Borders, or the lip-smacking Yum Yum, a sausage-shaped doughnut. But you don't get more Scottish than Irn Bru, so why not whisk it into an orangy, bubbly mousse? Or tuck into a creamy, purple Heather Rice. Highland raspberries are among the best in the world, so mix them with honey made by busy Scottish bees. Or try a sweet pancake, served with must-eat-more butterscotch sauce.

Condensed milk is always a favourite and I used to eat it on a slice of bread. My dentist didn't thank me and yours won't either – and no healthy person will want more than one Deep-Fried Mini Mars Bar in a lifetime – but they are rather scrummy. Never mind, there's always good old Trifle – and in the old days, every house had its own version, usually inspired by Granny. We make ours with chocolate; in Scotland, if someone's vain they say: 'If he were chocolate, he'd eat himself!'

Heather Rice

The time to have this is when the heather hits the hills ... You can, of course, eat it all year round – the September colours just remind us what a scrummy pudding it is.

(Serves 4–6)

50g/2oz pudding rice
570 ml/1 pint milk
40g/1$\frac{1}{2}$ oz sugar
25g/1oz butter
3 tbsp dark jam – blackberry/plum

Set the oven to Gas Mark 2/150˚ C. Use a slither of the butter to grease an ovenproof dish.

Put the rice and sugar into the dish and pour over the milk. Stir and dot with the remaining butter.

Bake in the oven for two hours, or until the rice is cooked.

Remove the skin from the pudding – but keep it as, for some folk, it's the best bit of all and now add the jam and stir carefully until purple.

WEE NOTES

Raspberry Creamie

More raspberries – mmm. To make this into a traditional Scottish 'crowdie' pudding, add a tablespoon of toasted medium oatmeal to the cream.

(Serves 4)

250g/9oz raspberries
4 dessertspoons of honey
75 ml/3fl oz double cream
75 ml/3fl oz plain yoghurt
50g/2oz soft brown sugar

Divide the raspberries between four dishes and drizzle a dessertspoon of honey over the top of each.

In a bowl whip the cream and fold in the yoghurt. Spread this over the fruit, then sprinkle the brown sugar on top.

Put in the fridge until the sugar melts into the cream.

WEE NOTES

Choc-Scots Trifle

What Scottish house doesn't have its own special trifle? Some come with raspberry jam; others with peaches and custard. This one is a chocolate delight and is ready in minutes.

(Serves 4)

1 x 85g shop-bought chocolate Swiss roll
1 small tin mandarin slices
3 fl oz/75 ml double cream
2 small cartons shop-bought chocolate mousse
Flaked chocolate or buttons for the top

Drain the tin of fruit. Whisk the cream until thick. Cut the Swiss roll into 12 rounds and divide between four sundae dishes. Arrange the mandarins over the cake. Spoon the chocolate mousse over that, add a dollop of cream and decorate with flaked chocolate or buttons.

WEE NOTES

Irn Bru Mousse

Irn Bru – it's a Scottish institution – what more can you say?! For Irn Bru Jelly, use three quarters of a pint of Irn Bru and leave out the milk.

(Serves 4–6)

275 ml/^{1}/$_2$ pint Irn Bru
1 x 11g sachet gelatine
2 tbsp fresh orange juice
1 tbsp water
1 small tin/170g evaporated milk

Pour the Irn Bru drink into a bowl to let the bubbles die down.

Put the orange juice and water into another bowl and sprinkle over the gelatine. Place that in a pan of hot water and heat gently until the gelatine is melted.

Strain the melted gelatine through a sieve into the Irn Bru, mixing all the time.

Add the evaporated milk and with an electric whisk, beat the mixture until very frothy. Pour into a dish and put in the fridge to set.

WEE NOTES

Pink Porridge

Real Scots eat their porridge with salt. But raspberries are equally Scottish and better for you.

(Serves 2–3)

275 ml/½ pint milk
110g/4oz medium porridge oats

2 tbsp raspberry jam
4 tbsp cold milk

Put the milk and oats into a saucepan and bring gently to the boil. Now turn down the heat and simmer for three minutes. Remove from the stove and mix in the raspberry jam.

Serve with a tablespoon of cold milk over the top.

WEE NOTES

Marmalade Pears

Is marmalade good for you? It was said that Mary, Queen of Scots ate it when she became seasick while travelling from France to Scotland in 1561. The first marmalade factory was built in Scotland more than 200 years ago. No-one likes thick peel, so either use thin-cut marmalade – either orange or lime – or sieve out the bits of peel after melting the jam with the orange juice.

(Serves 4)

4 small firm pears
Juice from 2 oranges
4 tbsp marmalade

Put the marmalade into a saucepan with the orange juice and melt over a low heat. Peel the pears and pop them into the marmalade mixture.

Cover and simmer for 10 minutes, or until the fruit is tender.

Serve with ice-cream.

WEE NOTES

Banoffee Toffee Pies

The name is good enough to eat. This dish was first made in Britain in the early 1970s and is now eaten all over the world. And no wonder – it is very moreish. Remember, if you're cooking together, the adult should do the 'hot' bits.

(Serves 6)

220g/1 small tin condensed milk
175g/6oz digestive biscuits
40g/1$\frac{1}{2}$ oz butter
2 small bananas
150 ml/5fl oz double cream

Put the tin of condensed milk, unopened, into a pan of water, bring to the boil and simmer very gently for about one-and-a-half hours. Keep it covered with water all the time. When you take it out, cool before opening. The result should be a tin of cold, soft toffee.

Meanwhile, line 6 x 7 cm/3 inch muffin tins with foil, leaving an inch of foil over the sides. This will help you to lift the puddings out later.

Crush the biscuits into crumbs by putting them into a bag and bashing with a rolling pin. Melt the butter and mix with the crushed biscuits. Divide this mix between the tins and press down firmly to make the pudding base.

Peel and thinly slice the bananas and divide them between the biscuit bases. Then spoon the toffee mix over the bananas.

Finally, whip the cream until firm and divide between the dishes. Put in the fridge for half an hour. Lift the pies out, remove the foil and serve.

WEE NOTES

Please note: Before heating the tin of condensed milk (see opposite), you must make sure that the top of the tin is pierced several times. Place it in a pan of water so that three-quarters of the tin is submerged. Be sure to keep the water topped up while the tin simmers, as it will evaporate.

Scotch Pancakes

The food writer, Catherine Brown, used to make pancake 'people' – 'great, fat, sprawling figures' that filled the pancake pan. Make yours as round or as ragged as you want.

(Serves 4–6)

110g/4oz self-raising flour
50g/2oz caster sugar
1 egg
2 tbsp milk
25g/1oz butter for frying

Sift the flour and add the caster sugar. Then whisk in the egg and milk. You want a smooth, thick batter with no lumps.

Heat a frying pan and melt a little butter. Drop in separate tablespoonfuls of the batter and cook until you see the tops bubbling. Then turn over and cook the other side.

Eat with bananas, syrup or butterscotch sauce (see opposite page).

WEE NOTES

Butterscotch Sauce

This is just about the yummiest sauce imaginable! It keeps well for a week or so in a screw-top jar stored in a cool place.

50g/2oz butter
150g/5oz brown sugar
5 tbsp syrup
75 ml/3 fl oz double cream

Put the butter, sugar and syrup into a pan and heat slowly until the sugar melts. This should take about five minutes.

Allow to cool slightly and add the double cream.
Stir well and serve hot or cold.

WEE NOTES

Bramble Fooleries

225g/8oz brambles (blackberries)
50g/2oz sugar
150 ml/$^1/_4$ pint ready-made custard
150 ml/$^1/_4$ pint double cream

Put the brambles and the sugar into a pan over a low heat on the stove.

When soft, cool slightly and blend – either in a processor, or with a masher. Sieve and mix the purée with the custard. Lightly whip the cream and add that too.

It looks better if you don't mix it too much – so there are streaks of purple, yellow and white.

Serve in glass dishes.

WEE NOTES

Apple and Jam Frushie

A frushie is something crumbly — hence the pastry. Use any fruit or jam you like.

(Serves 6)

350g/12oz apples
225g/8oz shortcrust pastry
3 tbsp raspberry jam
50g/2oz caster sugar

Set the oven to Gas Mark 6/200° C.
Roll out half of the pastry and line a
20cm/7 inch flan dish.

Peel, core and slice the apples and place on the
pastry, spread the jam over the top, then
sprinkle with the sugar. Cover with the
remaining pastry. Seal the pie edges with water
and pinch together.

Make a slit in the top and bake for 30–35
minutes.

WEE NOTES

BAKING

The Scots have always been great bakers; from their Tattie Scones to their Buttery Rowies (a butter-rich bread roll). And what baker's shop doesn't have a row of fat pink and white-topped Cookies in its window? These are not like the American Cookies, which are flat biscuits; Scottish Cookies are sweet bread rolls covered in icing. If you bake some of the delicious recipes in this section, you could invite your friends round for a party, or a 'Cookie Shine'.

Poragies (or 5-4-3s)

Natasha and I discovered Poragies in a delightful Katie Morag storybook. The nice thing about these is that they're scrumptious and easy to make.

150g/5oz medium porridge oats
110g/4oz butter
75g/3oz soft brown sugar

Pre-heat the oven to Gas mark 5/190° C.
Grease an 18 x 27 cm/8 x 11 inch tin.

Melt the butter in a pan, then stir in the oats and sugar and mix well. Allow to cool slightly.

Press the mixture into the tin and bake for 12-15 minutes or until golden brown. Cut into slices whilst still warm.

WEE NOTES

Orange Shorties

Shortbread is so Scottish. This buttery, crumbly biscuit takes on a new twist with the addition of the orange. If you want to be daring, you could also add a small packet of chocolate drops.

110g/4oz plain flour, sieved
50g/2oz cornflour, sieved
25g/1oz caster sugar
25g/1oz icing sugar, sieved
110g/4oz butter

Finely grated peel of one orange

Pre-heat the oven to
Gas Mark 2/150° C.
Grease a 27 x 18cm/8 x 11 inch oblong tin or an 18cm/8 inch round tin.

Mix the flour, cornflour and the sugars. Rub in the butter until you have fine crumbs. Then add the finely grated orange peel.

Press firmly into the greased tin and bake for 40-50 minutes, or until lightly browned.

Cut into pieces whilst still warm and leave to cool in the tin.

WEE NOTES

Chocolate Snowballs

You can buy these in the shops – they're all biscuity, chocolatey and coconuty. Home-made, they're even more delicious. So, keep them coming!

15 digestive biscuits
2 tbsp drinking chocolate
220g/1 small tin condensed milk
110g/4oz dessicated coconut
50g/2oz butter

Crush the biscuits by putting them in a bag and bashing them with a rolling pin. Put the crumbs into a bowl, then add the drinking chocolate, condensed milk and two thirds of the coconut. Then melt the butter and mix everything together.

When the mixture is cool enough to handle, roll it into small sweetie-sized balls and coat with the remaining coconut. Put in the fridge to set.

WEE NOTES

Fudgies

There's no doubt, the Scots love their sweets and biscuits. These are scrumptious, but very sugary, so don't forget to brush your teeth ...

110g/4oz caster sugar
220g/1 small tin condensed milk
110g/4oz butter
1 tbsp syrup

450g/1lb shortbread biscuits

Grease a 28 x 18 cm/11 x 7 inch baking tin.

Put the sugar, condensed milk, butter and syrup into a pan and slowly bring to the boil. Simmer for three minutes, stirring so the mixture doesn't catch the bottom of the pan. Put the biscuits in a bag and bash them with a rolling pin until you have big crumbs. Then add them to the pan and mix everything together.

With a spoon, press the mixture into the greased tin. Cool slightly, put in the fridge and cut into squares when set.

WEE NOTES

Tottie Buns

Tottie means small and these little buns go really well with raspberries from the Scottish Highlands. They're easy to make and they're very moreish.

225g/8oz self-raising flour
110g/4oz margarine
75g/3oz caster sugar
1 egg
1 tbsp milk
4 tbsp raspberry jam

Pre-heat the oven to Gas Mark 5/190˚ C. Grease a large, flat baking tin with a slither of the margarine.

Sift the flour into a bowl. Rub the margarine into the flour until you have fine crumbs. Stir in the caster sugar. Beat the egg and the milk together and gradually add this to the bowl. It should be firmer than a cake mix, but not too dry. If it seems too crumbly, add a teaspoon or so of extra milk.

Put some flour on your hands and roll the mixture into balls, each the size of a small plum. You should have about 16.

Place each ball at least an inch apart on the tray. With your finger, make a hole in the top.

Fill each hole with a quarter of a teaspoon of jam and bake for about 15-20 minutes, or until risen and golden brown.

WEE NOTES

Gingerbread Men

110g/4oz plain flour
1 tsp ground ginger
1 tsp bicarbonate soda
50g/2oz margarine
50g/2oz soft brown sugar
50g/2oz syrup
A few currants/nuts/cherries for decoration
A little extra flour for rolling out.

Gingerbread man cutter.
Pre-heat oven to Gas Mark 5/190° C.
Grease a large baking tray.

Sift the flour, ginger and bicarbonate of soda into a bowl. Rub the margarine into the flour mixture, then add the sugar. Add the syrup and using your hands, gather it all together into a pastry.

Roll the mixture out on a floured surface and cut gingerbread shapes with a cutter.

Place on the baking tray, leaving plenty of room between each biscuit. Add currants/nuts/cherries for eyes and a mouth.

Bake for 10-15 minutes, or until golden brown. Cool on the tray for 10 minutes before lifting off.

WEE NOTES

St Andrew's Cakes

St Andrew is the patron saint of Scotland and the St Andrew's flag, the Saltire, is a blue cross on a white background. Serve these at a party on St Andrew's Day – 30 November.

110g/4oz soft margarine
110g/4oz caster sugar
2 eggs
110g/4oz self-raising flour
1 tbsp milk

175g/6oz icing sugar
Water to mix
1 x 250g packet ready-to-roll white icing
Blue food colouring
A little jam

Set the oven to Gas Mark 5/190° C.
Put 12 paper cake cases into a 12-bun tin.

Beat the margarine and the sugar together until soft, then add the eggs and the flour and mix well. Add the milk and stir round again.

Divide the mixture between the paper cases and bake in the oven for 12–15 minutes, or until golden and they spring back when you touch the tops. Take out of the oven and cool.

Make the white icing by sieving the icing sugar into a bowl and mixing it with two to three teaspoons of water. Ice the tops of the cakes and allow to set.

Take the ready-to-roll icing and add a few drops of blue colouring until you have blue icing. Roll out thinly and cut 24 strips, each 6 cm x $2^{1}/_{2}$ cm. Form them into crosses on the white icing to make the flag of St Andrews. Use a bit of jam to make them stick.

WEE NOTES

WEE TREATS

For most Wee Macs this is the best bit of all; making the small, sweet bites that get gobbled up in no time. The Scots have some wonderful names for their sweeties. Nuttie Glessie is a hard, sticky, nut-filled toffee and you really must get your tongue round a minty Hawick Ball ... Our favourite is the Chocolate Hedgehog — and when it's summer we chill with refreshing fruity lollies and Lemon Barley Drink.

Tablet

Tablet is as Scottish as Haggis – and probably more popular! You can vary the flavourings using lemon or peppermint essence – but we like it just the way it is.

110g/4oz butter
900g/2lb sugar
1 tbsp syrup
150 ml/$\frac{1}{4}$ pint of milk
A few drops vanilla essence
Butter for greasing

Grease a 20 x 28 cm/8 x 11 inch tin with butter.

In a heavy-bottomed, high-sided pan, put the butter, sugar, syrup and milk. Stir, bring gently to the boil and continue boiling for 20 minutes stirring from time to time to stop it from sticking. Take off the heat and add the vanilla essence. Allow to cool for a few minutes; then beat well with a wooden spoon, or use an electric whisk for five minutes. Be careful as the mixture will still be hot!

Pour into the tin. When cool, cut into squares.

WEE NOTES

Honey Raspberry Lollies

Again, two very Scottish ingredients. Think of all those bees gathering pollen to make honey just for you! The sweetness of that and the sharpness of the raspberries works very well.

150g/5oz raspberries
2 tbsp runny honey
150 ml/¼ pint water

Put the raspberries, honey and water into a liquidiser and blend until you have a smooth purée. Then strain into a jug and pour into lolly moulds.

Freeze for at least two hours.

WEE NOTES

Lemon Barley Water

This is refreshing after doing a lot of exercise on a long, hot day. True, we don't get many of those in Scotland, but we can dream!

50g/2oz pearl barley
600 ml/1 pint water
1 lemon
2 tbsp honey

Put the barley in a sieve and rinse it with water. Then put it in a pan with the water. Grate the rind from the lemon and add that to the barley mixture. Bring to the boil on the stove, and simmer for half an hour. Take off the stove and allow to cool slightly.

Strain the liquid into a jug – you don't need the barley now. Squeeze the juice from the lemon and mix that in along with the honey.

Serve with ice-cubes.

WEE NOTES

Quick Raspberry Jam

There's nothing like home-made jam, but be careful – hot jam can give a nasty burn, so make sure the adult does all the difficult bits.

450g/1lb raspberries
450g/1lb caster sugar

(Makes 2 jars)

Warm two clean jam jars. Put the raspberries and sugar into a heavy-bottomed pan and bring slowly to the boil. Stir and simmer for eight minutes. Pour into the jars. Place a waxed disc over the top and put the lids on.

Eat within a month. When open, keep in the fridge.

WEE NOTES

Deep-Fried Mini Mars Bars

Yes these do exist! Try them once. You will either love or hate them. Again, make sure the adult does the 'hot' bits.

8 mini Mars bars
50g/2oz plain flour
1 egg
15g/^{1}/$_2$ oz caster sugar
65 ml/2^1/$_2$ fl oz milk
Vegetable oil for frying

Make a batter by mixing the flour, egg, sugar and milk until smooth and lump-free.

Put the oil on the stove to heat – you will need about 5 centimetres in the pan. The oil should be a temperature of 180˚ C (test by adding a small cube of bread to the pan. It should turn golden after a minute). Then dip a mini Mars bar into the batter and lower it carefully into the oil with a large, long handled spoon.

Cook for a few seconds until slightly browned, then take out with a slotted spoon. Drain on a paper towel. Repeat with the remaining Mars bars. Use any left-over batter to make sweet pancakes.

WEE NOTES

Chocolate Hedgehogs

Hedgehogs like Scotland – in some areas they're overrunning the place! This is a good Mrs Tiggy Winkle party sweet, with a lovely mix of biscuit, chocolate, marshmallow and fruit. You could add all sorts of things to the cocktail sticks, including wee sweeties ...

4 Tunnock's Teacakes
20 small grapes
20 tiny marshmallows
1 chocolate flake bar
A teaspoon of jam

You will also need 20 wooden cocktail sticks.

With a pair of scissors, cut the cocktail sticks in half. You should have 40 – and that's 10 for each teacake. To make your hedgehog, stick a mix of grapes and marshmallows onto the blunt end of each half stick and then very carefully push the sharp end of the sticks into the teacake to form the hedgehog 'prickles'. Cut a small piece of chocolate flake for the snout and stick it to the body with a dab of jam.

WEE NOTES

MY OWN RECIPE

MY OWN RECIPE

GLOSSARY

Aipple — apple

Arbroath smokie — a small haddock that's been salted and then smoked over a fire. It comes from the name of a port in east scotland

Ashet — a large dish, usually oval, used for serving food

Bannock — a round, flat cake, made from oats or barley

Bashit — mashed vegetables

Beastie — a small creature or insect — make sure your lettuce is well washed, we don't want beasties on it!

Black bun — a rich fruit cake

Bramble — blackberry

Bree — some soups are called bree, eg partan bree, which is a crab soup

Breid — the scots word for bread

Bridie — a pasty, filled with minced meat

Bubblyjock — turkey

Buttery — a butter-rich bread roll

Champit or chappit — mashed

Clootie dumpling — a rich fruit pudding, boiled in a cloth or cloot

Collop — a thin slice of meat fried in a pan

Cullen skink — a thick fish soup, made from smoked haddock and potatoes

Drap — drop

Drooth — thirst

Haddie — a haddock. Ham and haddie is a famous scottish dish

Haggis — a dish made of minced sheep liver, heart and lungs, mixed with suet and oatmeal and seasoning

Howtowdie – a dish made of chicken with spinach and poached eggs

Jeelie – jelly or jam

Kail or kale – a green, leafy vegetable

Kailyard – vegetable patch

Meat – not just meat, it can mean any sort of food

Messages – groceries

Oatcake – a thin, savoury oat biscuit

Piece – a sandwich

Piecebox – a sandwich box

Pottit heid – the head of an animal which has been cooked, chopped and covered in jelly

Queenie – a large scallop

Roasted cheese – cheese on toast

Rowie – a bread roll

Rumbledethump – a dish of vegetables and potatoes

Shortie – shortbread biscuit

Skirlie – a dish of oatmeal and onions

Stovie – a dish of sliced potatoes and onions

Sweetie – a sweet

Tablet – a sweet, like fudge

Tattie – potato

Tumshee – turnip

Yum-yum – a long doughnut-type cake

INDEX

Apple   23, 55
Apple and Jam Frushie   55
Auld Alliance (French Toast)   10
Bacon   22
Banana   50
Banoffee Toffee Pies   50
Beefburger   26
Bits 'n' Pieces   1
Blackberries/ brambles   54
Bramble Fooleries   54
Bread   8, 10
    Breadcrumbs   34
    Bread rolls   26
    Brown bread   4
    Butterscotch sauce   53
Cabbage   23, 24
Carrot   7, 11, 18,
20, 24, 26
Cheese   32, 34
    Cheddar cheese   8
    Cottage cheese   6
    Cream cheese   6
    Parmesan cheese   2, 32
Cheese Patties   32
Chicken   34
Chicken breast   25
Chicken drumsticks   19
Children's Cock-a-Leekie   25
Chocolate
    Chocolate Flake Bar   77
    Chocolate mousse   46
    Chocolate Snowballs   62
    Drinking Chocolate   62
Chocolate Hedgehogs   77
Choc-Scots Trifle   46
Coconut   62
Corned beef   5
Cranberry jelly   36
Deep-Fried Mini Mars Bars   76
Digestive biscuit   50, 62
Egg   7, 10,
28, 30
    Quails' egg   16, 30
Fish   29
    Salmon   29
    Tuna   7

Smoked haddock   16
Smoked mackerel   6
Smoked Mackerel Dip   1, 6
Smoked salmon   viii, 4
Smoked Salmon Wheels   1, 4
French Toast   10
Fudgies   63
Gingerbread Men   65
Grapes   77
Green beans   18
Haggis   28, 38
Haggis Tatties   38
Ham   34
Heather Rice   44
Honey   45, 73, 74
Honey Raspberry Lollies   73
Irn Bru Jelly   47
Irn Bru Mousse   47
Jam   44, 48,
55, 64
    Quick Raspberry Jam   75
Kid's Kedgeree   16
Leeks   25
Lemon Barley Water   74
Lettuce   7, 26
Macaroni   8
Marmalade Pears   49
Mars Bar   76
Marshmallows   77
Mayonnaise   7, 23, 26
Meat   34
Mince 'n' Tatties   20
Mini Mac Pies   8
Neeps 'n' Tattie Nests   28
Nourishing Soup   11
Oatcakes   2, 6
Oatie Drummers   19
Oatmeal   30, 32
Oats   19
    Porridge oats   48, 60
Orange
    Orange juice   47, 49
    Orange peel   61
    Orange Shorties   61
Pancake men   5
Patties   32

Pear   49
Pearl barley   36, 74
Peas   24
Pink Porridge   48
Pizza Oaties   2
Poragies (or 5-4-3s)   60
Pork sausage meat   30
Potatoes   5, 20, 22,
24, 25, 28, 32, 33
    Baking potato   38
    Green Champit   33, 36
Prunes   25
Pudding rice   44
Raspberry   45, 73, 75
    Quick Raspberry Jam   75
    Raspberry Creamie   45
    Raspberry Jam   48, 55. 64
Red and White Salad   23
Red lentils   11
Roastit Bubblyjock
        with Barley   36
Rumbledethumps   24
Scotch Beef   20, 26
Scotch Pancakes   52
See you Jimmy Heids
        (Egg Heads)   7
Shortbread   63
Sit There Pie   34
St Andrews Cakes   66
Stovies   22
Swiss Roll   46
Tablet   72
Tattie Hash Waffles   5
Tomato   7, 26
Tomato pasta sauce   2
Tottie Buns   64
Tottie Fish Suppers   29
Trifle   43
Tunnock's Teacakes   77
Turkey   36
Turnip   18, 28, 38
Wee Meaty Macs   26
Wee Scotch Eggs   30
White Neep Salad   18
White rice   16
Yoghurt   45